michael bublécomeflywithme

piano vocal guitar

michaelbublécomeflywithme

© International Music Publications
Music arranged and engraved by Artemis Music Ltd

Published 2004
© International Music Publications
Music arranged and engraved by Artemis Music Ltd

nice 'n easy

words by alan bergman and marilyn keith
music by lewis spence

Let's_ take it nice and ea - sy,___ it's_ gon -na be
Hey_ ba - by what's your hur - ry?___ Re - lax and don't

_ so ea - sy___ for_ us to fall in love._
_ you wor - ry,___ we're_____

To Coda ✛

To rush would be_____ a crime,_____ 'cause_____

_____ nice and ea - sy does it ev - 'ry time._____

nice and ea - sy does it, nice and ea - sy

does it, nice and ea - sy does it___ ev - ry time.___

(Spoken): "One more time."

can't help falling in love

words and music by george weiss, hugo peretti and luigi creatore

my funny valentine

words and music by richard rodgers and lorenz hart

mack the knife

words by berthold brecht
music by kurt weill
translation by marc blitzstein

fever

words and music by john davenport and eddie cooley

Verse 5:
Now you've listened to my story,
Here's the point that I have made
Chicks were born to give you fever
Be it Fahrenheit or centigrade
They give you fever
When you kiss them, fever if you live and learn
Fever, till you sizzle
What a lovely way to burn...

you'll never know

words by mack gordon
music by harry warren

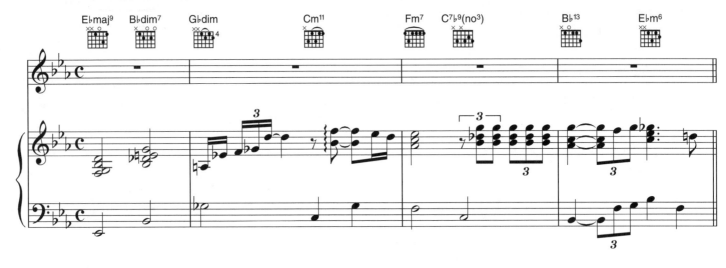

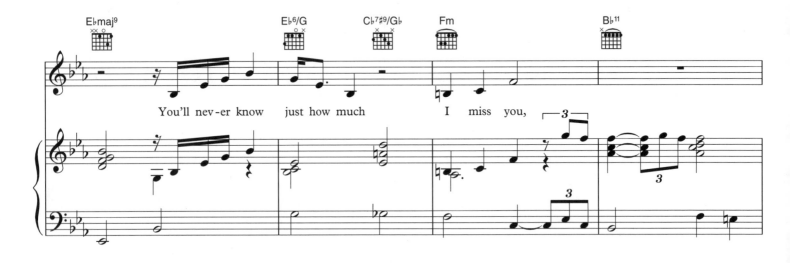

You'll nev-er know   just how much   I miss you,

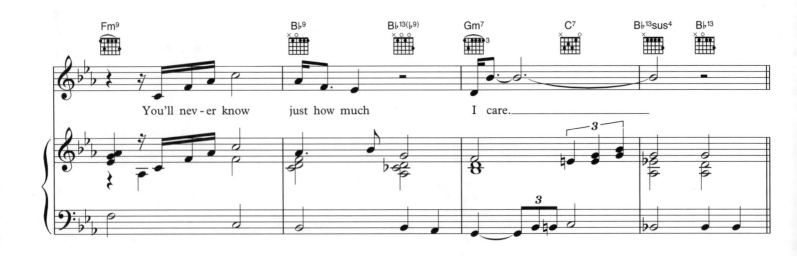

You'll nev-er know   just how much   I care.

for once in my life

words by ronald miller
music by orlando murden

moondance

words and music by van morrison

1. mar-ve-lous night___ for a moon-dance___ with the stars___ up a-bove in your eyes..

2. 3. wan-na make love___ to you to-night,___ I can't wait___ till the morn-ing has come.

come fly with me

words by sammy cahn
music by james van heusen

kissing a fool

words and music by george michael

sway

words and music by ruiz beltran
english translation by norman gimbel

start to play,___ dance with me,___ make me sway.___ Like a la-zy o-cean
in the breeze,___ bend with me,___ sway with ease.___ When we dance you got a

When ma-rim-ba rhy-thms

that's all

words and music by bob haymes and alan brandt

D.%.al Coda

-fold you___ and a love time could nev - er___ de - stroy. If you're

Coda

(Saxophone solo ad. lib)

all.

If___

___ you're won-d'ring what I'm ask - ing in re - turn dear, you'll be

Verse 3:

If you're wondering what I'm asking in return dear,
You'll be glad to know that my demands are small.
Say it's me that you'll adore
For now and evermore,
That's all,
That's all.

how can you mend a broken heart

words and music by barry gibb and robin gibb

the way you look tonight

words by dorothy fields
music by jerome kern

Verse 3:
Lovely, never, ever change.
Keep that breathless charm.
Won't you please arrange it?
'Cause I love you
Just the way you look tonight.

Verse 4:
(Instrumental)